THE ULTIMATE BOOK OF

CHALLENGING RIDDLES

FOR KIDS!

AGES 8-12

AC BROOKER

FREE BONUS

SCAN THE QR CODE TO GET OUR NEXT BOOK MAILED TO YOU FOR FREE!

TABLE OF CONTENTS

AC BROOKER

GET YOUR RIDDLE HATS ON!

Solving riddles trains your brain, similar to how sports train your body. And it's equally important! Riddles allow children to think outside the box, and use both logic and creativity to solve them!

Don't be discouraged if you don't get the answer right away – that's the point of this book! It will help you train your brain and get better at riddles with each one you do solve!

Here are a few tips:
- Take your time! The riddles aren't going anywhere. Really read the question slowly and thoroughly if you need to, to really be sure of what it's asking.
- Guess a lot where needed! Sometimes ruling out the wrong answers will help you find the RIGHT ones!
- Be creative! Are there words that have more than one meaning in the question?

There's not much more to it than getting your riddle hat on, thinking outside the box, and solving your way through the book! Are you ready?

Good luck!

CHAPTER 1: RANDOM RIDDLES

1. What has to be broken before you can eat it?

_____

2. The names of a mother, father, son, and daughter are Finlay, Anna, Alex, and Genie. Alex and Anna are the same age, and Genie is almost 7 years old. What is the name of the son?

_____

3. Which word in the English alphabet both begins and ends with the letter "E" but only contains one letter?

_____

4. Which month of the year has at least 30 days?

_____

5. What can you catch but not throw?

_____

6. What becomes wetter the more it dries?

_____

7. What can carry so much food for you, but you can trust that it will never eat any of it?

_____

8. What twins live together all of the time, see the whole world but never see each other?

_____

9. A black bear is heavier than a dog. A polar bear is heavier than a black bear. A rhino is heavier than a polar bear. Which is lighter: a rhino or a black bear?

_____

10. Charlie was born in September and Jake was born in March. Who is older?

_____

11. What has hands and a face but can't hold anything?

_____

12. What's the capital in Spain?

_____

13. Which word becomes shorter when you add just two letters to it?

_____

14. What is the only word in the dictionary that is spelt incorrectly?

_____

15. If you drop your gloves in the dead sea what do they become?

_____

16. What is at the end of everything?

_____

17. What is mainly orange with a bit of green on top and and sounds like a parrot?

_____

18. What type of buildings have the most stories?

_____

19. What can't talk but will always reply?

_____

20. What falls a lot but doesn't get hurt?

_____

21. What is so fragile that if you say its name aloud you'll instantly break it?

_____

22. What has many words but never speaks?

_____

23. Which word contains 26 letters but only has 3 syllables?

_____

24. Name a vehicle which is spelt the same forwards as backwards?

_____

25. If you feed me air I will grow, but please don't give me water or else I will die. What am I?

_____

26. What is made purely of water but if you put it in water it will disappear?

_____

27. A boy fell off a 30-foot ladder but wasn't hurt at all and simply laughed. How could this be?

_____

28. What starts with the letter "P", ends with an "E", and has thousands of letters?

_____

29. What is in seasons, seconds, centuries, and minutes but not in decades, years, or days?

_____

30. How many animals did Moses take on the ark?

_____

31. Name something you can put in your pocket that will keep it empty?

_____

32. What has 13 hearts but no other organs?

_____

33. What is forever in front of you but can never be seen?

_____

34. What is a tasty food that stalks the countryside with ears but can't see?

_____

35. What 4 letter word can be written either forwards of backwards and even upside down and can still be read from left to right correctly?

_____

36. What word is pronounced exactly the same even if you take away the last two letters from it?

_____

37. What kind of band never plays any music?

_____

38. What has towns, cities, villages, landmarks but no people?

_____

39. What is a load of rubbish but very useful for us humans in fact everyone will have one of these?

_____

40. What can you hold in your left hand but it is impossible to hold in your right hand?

_____

41. Your grandpa went out for a walk, but forgot his umbrella or a hat. It started to rain heavily, but when he got back there wasn't a hair on his head that got wet. He was outside the whole time. How was this possible?

_____

42. Very few people have ever stepped on me and not for a long time. Maybe it's because I have a dark side. I'm occasionally full but not for long. What am I?

_____

43. Name something that can't be put in a saucepan.

_____

44. Where do two walls meet each other?

_____

45. I make a popping sound when I'm hot. When I pop, I change but I get lighter. What am I?

_____

46. What starts with a "T", ends with a "T" and is also full of "T"?

_____

47. What runs all day and all night but never gets hot?

_____

48. Add 1 letter to the number "one" to make it disappear?

_____

49. What always stays in the corner but can travel all around the world?

_____

50. What has keys but no locks, space but not room and you can enter but not leave?

_____

51. A man holds $10.25 in his hand but only has one coin. How is this possible?

_____

52. What is a frog's favorite game to play?

_____

53. What's a house's favorite item of clothing to wear?

_____

54. Give one good reason why the fly was very afraid of ever landing on the computer?

_____

55. Name an animal that is great with letters and is smarter than a talking parrot?

_____

56. What kind of breakfast murderer is full of fibre?

_____

57. What kind of running leads to walking? (Think cars!)

_____

58. Why is the letter "A" always afraid of flowers?

_____

59. What do you call an adventurous snail taking charge of a ship?

_____

60. Why did the poor skeleton go alone to the party?

_____

CHAPTER 2: WHO AM I?
WHAT AM I?

1. Children love to make a lot of this but no one including themselves can see it. What is it?

_____

2. I have both a head and a tail but no body. What am I?

_____

3. When I left, I thought I was going east, thanks to the wind. When I arrived, I didn't know where I was, and when I returned, I didn't know where I had been. Who am I?

_____

4. This belongs solely to you but you'll often find other people using it a lot more than you ever do. What is it?

_____

5. I am one word. My first 4 letters describe everything that is alive today. My last 5 letters will watch over and protect you. Which word am I?

_____

6. They appear at night without anyone putting them there and they are lost in the day but are never stolen. What are they?

_____

7. When I'm squeezed I lose most of my weight. What am I?

_____

8. I saw a creature as white as anything, apart from his stick thin arms. He stood there still in the cold, but he himself was certainly not cold. When the sun came out he quickly disappeared. What could I have seen?

_____

9. I go from A to G. Sometimes I feel flat and other times I am sharp. What am I?

_____

10. When it comes to me, you go on red and stop on green. What am I?

_____

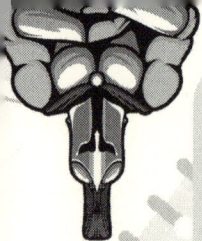

11. Thousands of brave soldiers lay gold in this amazing house but it's certainly not man-made. If you enter this house, you may just get a sweet surprise. What is it?

_____

12. I go round and round and move wherever someone pushes me. Some might say I'm the most important invention ever. What am I?

_____

13. I am a 5-letter word. Take away the first two letters and I become the opposite for the 5-letter word. Take away my first letter and I am a country. What am I?

_____

14. I like to copy others but I'm no primate. I'm often a shade of green but can be very colorful. What am I?

_____

15. They have neither feathers nor flesh, nor scales nor bones nor hair. But they do have fingers and thumbs of their own. What are they?

_____

16. Tomorrow I will be with you twice, yesterday you will find me only once but today I am gone. What am I?

_____

17. I'm usually white and used for cutting and grinding. When I'm damaged I either get filled in or taken out completely. What am I?

_____

18. I am only made of water but I'm not wet. What am I?

_____

19. I'm so simple that I can only point, but I have guided humans all over the world. What am I?

_____

20. Four legs up, four legs down, soft in the middle but hard all around. What am I?

_____

21. If you don't keep me, I'm almost certain to break. What am I?

_____

22. The older I get, the shorter I become, but I am not a human. Some say towards the end my life I look burnt out. What am I?

_____

23. People make me, save me, change me, raise me. What am I?

_____

24. I dig out caves and I fill the caves with gold and silver. I also sometimes build bridges of silver and make crowns of gold. At some point, everyone will need my help, yet many people will be afraid of the help I give. Who am I?

_____

25. I shave every day but my beard always stays the same length. What am I?

_____

26. People buy me to eat but never actually end up eating me. What am I?

_____

27. You answer me but I never ask any questions. What am I?

_____

28. I'm a god, a planet, and also a measure of heat. What am I?

_____

29. The more you take away from this, the bigger it becomes. What is it?

_____

30. I have 4 super strong legs but still cannot walk. What am I?

_____

31. I have no life but I sure can die on you. What am I?

_____

32. I have large wings but I am not a bird, yet I am able to fly very high up in the sky. What am I?

_____

33. I can't walk but prefer to run and I go with the flow most of the time. What am I?

_____

34. You see me once in June, twice in November, and never in May. What am I?

_____

35. I'm actually a seed with 3 letters to my name. If you take away the last letter or the last two letters I sound exactly the same. What am I?

_____

36. You are always cool when you're near me, thanks to my hands which wave at you. What am I?

_____

37. I'm always in you, sometimes on you, and if I surround you, I can kill you. What am I?

_____

38. I've got a very special skill. I can make two people out of one, but please be gentle with me. I can hurt you if you break me. What am I?

_____

39. Some people love me, some people hate me. I can change people's appearances and thoughts. If people take care of themselves, my value will increase. Some people try to hide me, but given enough time, I will show. No matter what people do or how hard they try I will never go down. What am I?

_____

40. My life is often measured in hours, but in my short life I will try to light up any room. Thin I will be quick, fat I will be slower. Wind is my foe. What am I?

_____

41. This is truly as light as a feather but no man nor woman can hold it for that long. What is it?

_____

42. I can both be told and played. I can both be cracked and made. What am I?

_____

43. I have no feet, no legs, no arms, and no hands, and I also have no wings. But I can climb high in the sky when you heat me up. What am I?

_____

44. I am very young but I have a little house all to myself. There are no windows or doors, so if I want to get out I must break through the wall. What am I?

_____

45. I am a 6 letter word. My last 3 would describe an animal you keep in your house, and another name for my first 3 is an automobile. What am I?

_____

46. You can touch me and break me. You should win me if you want to be mine. What am I?

_____

47. I reach high for the sky but remain firmly fastened to the ground. Sometimes I leave but I am always around. What am I?

_____

48. I run around the entire length of the field but never move. What am I?

_____

49. It really doesn't matter how much or how little you use me, you change me every month. What am I?

_____

50. I'm so strong I can damage ships, but I'm scared of the sun alright. What am I?

_____

51. I am a 6 letter word. When you take one letter away I become 12. What word am I?

_____

52. I have a very slender body, a tiny eye, and I'm sharp to the point. I'm a useful tool to help make clothes. What am I?

_____

53. I'm living tall and proud and then suddenly I am chopped. You place a skirt around my bottom. On the other end I am topped with an angel or a star. What am I?

_____

54. I have a back and legs, I can't move, and I certainly don't have any hair. What am I?

_____

55. Despite my name, I am no king nor queen. When you hold me against anything, their length is quickly seen. What am I?

_____

24

56. I can be red, green, or black and along with my buddies have a vine. I get picked and squeezed to make raisins, juice, or wine. What am I?

_____

57. I supply milk and I have a horn but I am no cow. What am I?

_____

58. I am often full of hundreds of wheels, but once I'm in position I never move. Part of my name is a lot. What am I?

_____

59. I'm very clean but the wetter I get the smaller I shrink. What am I?

_____

60. I always come on a roll but I'm not a kitchen towel. I'm usually clear but I'm not glass. I keep things together and I'm especially helpful at Christmas. You don't want me to get on your skin because I might take a few hairs off. What am I

_____

CHAPTER 3: MATH RIDDLES

1. When Lucy was 10, her brother was half her age. Lucy is now 16 years old, how old is his brother?

_____

2. Two fathers and two sons went out for the day fishing on the river. They caught 6 fish which meant there was enough for 2 fish each. How is this possible?

_____

3. Which is heavier: A ton of metal, a ton of feathers, or a ton of plastic?

_____

4. Liam has a very big family indeed. He has 15 aunts and uncles and 60 cousins. Every one of his cousins has an aunt that Liam doesn't have. How is this possible?

_____

5. My number is odd but if you take away just one letter I become even. What number am I?

_____

6. Charlotte was 9 the day before yesterday but next year she will turn 12. How is this possible?

_____

7. Mrs. Jackson has a very large family. She has 6 sons and each of her sons have two sisters. How many children does Mrs. Jackson have?

_____

8. It's currently midnight and it's snowing outside. Jules checks the weather forecast and sees for the next two days there will be clear weather without a cloud in the sky. 24 hours later Jules looks outside and she can't see the sun. How is this possible?

_____

9. You are cooking a lovely meal for your family. You have chopped up some potatoes into a bowl, ready to make some yummy fries! You count there are 25 chunks of potatoes in the bowl. You take 5 chunks out of the bowl. How many potato chunks do you have?

_____

10. What can you put in between 5 and 8 which would make the resulting number greater than 5 but less than 7?

---

11. A brand new clothing shop has a rather strange way of pricing their items. A belt costs $20, pants cost $25, a Blazer costs $30 and a tie costs $15. How much would shoes cost?

---

12. A rival clothing store has recently opened up and saw the success of their competitor with their unique pricing strategy. This store has also adopted a new unique pricing method. Here are what the same items cost. A belt costs $16, pants cost $18, a blazer costs $28 and a tie costs $22. How much would a pair of shoes cost?

---

13. 81 X 9 = 801. What do you need to do in order to make this equation correct?

---

14. What 3 numbers give the same number when they are multiplied or added together?

---

15. Double this number and then multiply it by 4. Then divide this new number by 8 and you'll have it once more. What number is it?

---

16. Let's say you have 3 chickens who lay eggs at a constant rate of 3 eggs between them, every 3 hours. How many chickens do you need to produce 700 eggs in 700 hours?

---

17. How can you make 45 using only the number 4? You can use as many 4s as you need! Think addition, subtraction, division, and multiplication.

---

18. I say that 6 + 7 = 1. How can that be possible?

---

19. What if I tell you that you can multiply any number in the world by THIS number and always get the same answer. What is this number?

---

20. A very long 500-foot train is traveling at 500 feet per minute. It goes through a 500 foot tunnel. How long does it take for the entire train to pass through the tunnel?

_____

21. A wildlife ranger decides to give some pocket money to some of the local animals. He gives an ostrich $15, a spider $60, and a scorpion $60. How much would both the lion and tiger get?

_____

22. Peter is a historian and he loves Ancient Rome. He takes two from FIVE and ends up with four. How did he do this?

_____

23. Ben has 3 times as many apples as he does pears. He has half as many pears as he does melons. He has as many melons as there are months in the year. How many apples, pears and melons does Ben have?

_____

24. A cube has 3 of these, a circle has 2, and a point has 0. What are they?

_____

25. If you flip a coin 20 times in a row and 19 times it lands on heads and it only lands on tails once. What is the probability that the next flip will land on heads?

26. This is something which is round but definitely not a circle. It looks a bit like an egg. What is it?

27. What should you add to 66,666 to equal 600?

28. Which statement is correct; 13 + 19 = 33, OR 19 - 13 = 7, OR 19 + 13 = 33?

29. A not so clever farmer bought 1 rooster so he could sell eggs for $1.5 each. If a chicken lays 5 eggs per day, how much money will the farmer make in 1 week?

30. If you multiply all the numbers of your phone number pad together. What is the total number you'll get?

31. You order your favorite pizza to serve 8 people and each person gets 1 slice each. How many times do you need to cut the pizza to get 8 slices?

_____

32. If a dozen loaves of bread cost you $1.20. How many loaves of bread can you get for $10?

_____

33. Another clever farmer bought 3 female chickens and 2 female ducks. One of the chickens is very old and can only lay 1 egg every 3 days. The other 2 chickens are young and healthy and each can lay 2 eggs every single day. The ducks are young and healthy but both each lay 1 egg per day. The farmer will sell each egg he gets for $0.50. The farmer unfortunately breaks 3 of the eggs he collects. How much will the farmer make if he has the chickens for 9 days?

_____

34. Theodore was born in 1998 and in 1980 he was 18 years old. How could this be?

___

35. A slug is in a deep pit 40 meters deep. He is trying to get out of the pit. Every day he climbs 10 meters up the size of the pit but slides back 8 meters. How many days will it take him to get out of the pit?

___

36. I am a number that if you cut in half I will be nothing and if you turn me on my side I will be everything. What number am I?

___

37. What is half of 2, plus 2, plus 2, plus 2?

___

38. A TV and the remote controller cost $110 together. The TV cost $100 more than the controller, how much did the TV cost?

___

39. I am a 3-digit number. My second digit is 6 times greater than my first digit and my third digit is 5 less than my second digit. What number am I?

___

40. George and William loved playing tennis, so they decided to play several matches last week. They decided to play for burgers. The winner of each match would buy the other a burger but no burgers were purchased until the end of the week. If George and William had the same number of wins at any time those burgers were canceled. George won 5 matches (but no burgers) and Willam won 4 burgers. How many tennis matches were played?

41. Olivia was asked to paint numbers on her school lockers. There are 100 lockers in total which means she will have to paint every number from 0-100. How many times will she paint the number 8?

42. "How much does this bag of carrots weigh?" asked the customer. The grocer replies "3 times a dozen pounds, divided by 6". How much did the bag of carrots weigh?

43. Which weighs more; 32 ounces of sugar or 2 pounds of solid metal?

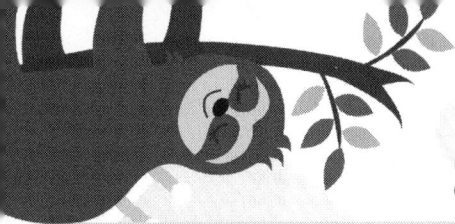

44. Sloths are very slow animals. Sid the sloth sleeps for 15 hours every day the rest of the time he slowly crawls. Sid crawls at a pace of 50 cm per hour. How many meters does Sid move in one full day?

_____

45. I am a 4 digit number. My fourth digit is the number 9. My second digit is half my third digit, and if you subtract 3 from my second digit, you will get my first digit. If you add 7 to my first digit, you will get my third digit. What is my number?

_____

46. If 4 men can build 4 chairs in 4 hours, how many chairs can 8 men build in 8 hours?

_____

47. Henry wants to go to the movies and will pay for his friends' tickets. Would it be cheaper for him to take one friend to the movie twice or two friends to the movie just once?

_____

48. Isabella goes shopping for some fruit and vegetables. She buys 20 melons, 120 grapes, 80 strawberries, 24 onions, and 6 potatoes. Unfortunately, 10% of the fruit got squished on the way home and 20% of the vegetables fell out of her grocery bag on the way back. How many total fruits and vegetables does she have left?

---

49. A bag of chocolate weighs one pound more than half of the weight of the bag. How much does the bag of chocolate weigh?

---

50. Pete is on a safari and is having a great time seeing loads of wild animals. He sees a pride of a dozen lions, a pack of 14 wild dogs, 2 ostriches and a herd of 98 wildebeest. He counted all the legs of every animal he saw. How many legs did he count?

---

51. I am smaller than 1/2 but bigger than 1/6 . My numerator is 1 and my denominator does not multiply to 25. What fraction am I?

---

52. If 88 = 4, 99 = 2, 6 = 1, 8086 = 6. What does 809689609 = ?

53. Take the number 100. Add just 1 number to it to make 1001 but that number can't be bigger than 100. How can you do this?

54. You are out shopping and want a new pair of shoes, a top, and a sweater. The shoes cost $40.50, the top costs $31.25, and the sweater costs $20. Your Mom said she'll pay for 50% of the shoes and the sweater, and you have to pay the rest. How much would you have to pay?

55. If it takes a man 40 minutes to walk 100 feet how long will he be able to walk in 10 hours?

56. A very large box contains 14 smaller boxes. Each of the smaller boxes contains 9 chocolate bars. Chantelle found that 1 of the smaller boxes only had 7 chocolate bars. How many chocolate bars were there total?

57. Sally can walk 4 kilometers in 1 hour. How many hours would it take her to walk 22km?

---

58. It usually takes Leroy 10 minutes to get ready for work in the morning. He then has to walk to his car which is parked around the corner from his house, and this is a 3 minute walk. His drive to work is 50 minutes and his walk from the car to his office is 19 minutes. Given that his car journey will be delayed by 10 minutes this morning, what time would he have to wake up in order to be at work for 8am?

---

59. A car manufacturer produced 2300 cars in their first year of production. 4500 cars were produced in their second year, and 550 more than the second year were produced in the third year. How many cars were produced in total?

---

60. Mo had $20 and needed more money to buy some food so he withdrew some money from his bank. He bought 3 bags of chips for $3 each, 2 whole chickens for $6 each, a bag of candy for $2.50, and two tubs of yogurt for $2.50 each. He was left with $15.50 after the paid for everything. How much did he withdraw from the bank?

CHAPTER 4: FUNNY RIDDLES

1. What can jump higher than a building?

_____

2. What's the best way to fix a scratched pumpkin?

_____

3. I was food once but you really shouldn't eat me. What am I?

_____

4. When things go very wrong what can you always count on?

_____

5. What do you call a chihuahua in the summer?

_____

6. What would you get if you happened to cross a snowman and a vampire?

_____

7. Teddy bears never seem to be hungry. Why is that?

_____

8. A Rhino in Africa is called Steph and a Rhino in Asia is called Stephanie. What is a Rhino in Antarctica called?

_____

9. Which one of Santa's reindeer is the fastest?

_____

10. Now I want you to imagine you are in a room with no windows and no doors. How will you get out?

_____

11. Why did the tortilla chip start dancing?

_____

12. What is the most expensive fish you could buy?

_____

13. A group of excited bunnies were at a party. What music were they listening to?

_____

14. What did the mommy tomato say to the slow-moving baby tomato?

_____

15. Where's the best place to take a sick boat?

_____

16. What did the triangle say to the circle?

_____

17. What type of room has no rooms, doors or windows?

_____

18. Why did the math book look so terrible?

_____

0 **19. What did the 0 say to the 8?** **8**

_____

20. What kind of beans won't grow in your garden but you can find them on easter?

_____

21. What did elves learn at school?

_____

22. What does the ghost use to wash his hair?

_____

23. Why is it dangerous to play cards in Africa? (Think big cats...)

_____

24. What is a tornado's favorite game to play?

_____

25. What is the best way for a scientist to freshen their breath?

_____

26. The nose was angry with the finger. What did the nose say to the finger?

_____

27. Why couldn't the pony sing a song today?

_____

28. Ducks are known for being very good detectives. Why do ducks make great detectives?

_____

29. Why didn't the apple win the race?

FINISH

_____

30. Name something that has four wheels and flies?

_____

31. What was the reason Mary threw the clock out of the window?

_____

32. What is the name given to a dinosaur that is sound asleep?

_____

33. Why did the silly pupil eat all of his homework?

_____

34. How do you spell CANDY in two letters?

_____

35. There were 5 boys and 2 girls walking to school. It had been raining all week and today they only had 1 umbrella between them. None of them got wet, how was this possible?

_____

36. What is the math teacher's favorite dessert?

_____

37. What kind of foods are the most fun at parties?

_____

38. Name something that tastes better than it smells?

_____

39. What has a bottom at their top?

_____

40. Why did Tigger want to go to the bathroom?

_____

46

CHAPTER 5: ANIMAL RIDDLES

1. How do you catch a school of fish?

_____

2. Which animal jumps when it walks and sits when it stands?

_____

3. I don't like sewing but I do have thousands of needles. What animal am I?

_____

4. Why did the fish blush?

_____

5. Why do dragons like to sleep all day?

_____

6. A cat can jump up to 3 meters high. There's a ground floor window which is 2 meters high. The cat tries to jump through but can't. Why can't the cat jump through?

_____

7. Cats love eating mice but will never go near this one type of mouse. What mouse am I talking about?

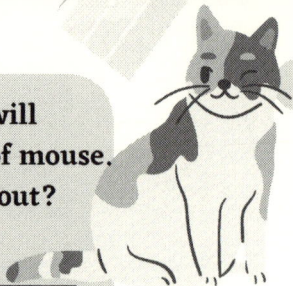

_____

8. Why do some fish prefer to live in saltwater?

_____

9. Why do cats make the best warriors?

_____

10. What's striped black and white and also blue?

_____

11. What did the hungry leopard say after finishing his meal?

_____

12. Why do reptiles and fish always manage to keep in such good shape?

13. Which animal is the best at baseball?

14. Where do fish sleep?

15. A horse walks a certain distance each day. Two of its legs walk 20 miles and its other two legs walk only 19 miles. The horse is normal and healthy, how is this possible?

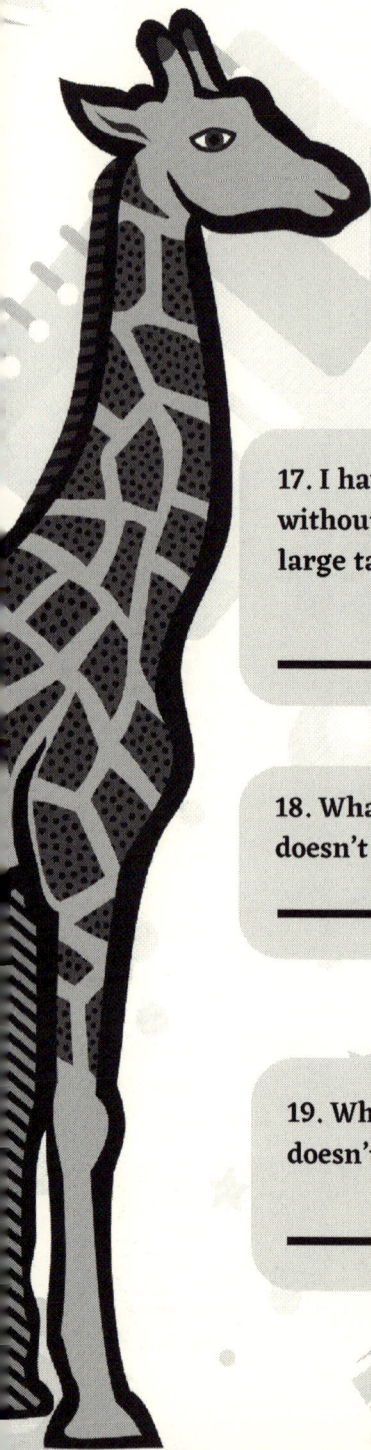

16. What two animal keys can't open a locked door?

_____

17. I have a hole in my back, I swim without using any legs and I have a large tail. What am I?

_____

18. What has an impressive horn but doesn't honk it?

_____

19. What's as big as a giraffe but doesn't weigh anything?

_____

20. A Lion, a Gorilla, and a Lizard are racing to the top of a pineapple tree. Who will get the apple first, the Lion, Gorilla, or the Lizard?

_____

21. What does the hungry horse reply to the waiter when the waiter greets him by saying 'hey'?

_____

22. My name is spelt very similar to a type of alcohol and my name rhymes with what mammals need to survive. What animal am I?

_____

23. How does a fight between two rival silkworms end?

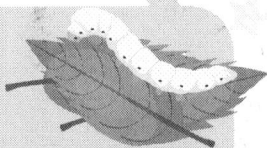

_____

24. What type of animal always has a buck?

_____

25. What did the bird say when the waiter brought her the check?

_____

26. What is the only mammal that cannot jump no matter how hard it tries?

_____

27. My head can't quite do a 360 but can certainly turn my head 270. I'm also noted for being fairly quiet when I'm gliding. What Am I?

_____

28. I'm pretty damn quick. In fact I've been clocked at 240 mph making me the fastest animal in the world. What am I?

_____

29. What animal has longer arms than legs and is thought to be 10X stronger than their body weight. Oh and has also been taught sign language?

_____

30. Which shop did the cat rush to when he noticed his tail had come off?

31. A girl stands on one side of the river and her dog is on the other side of the river. There is no bridge or boat to use but as soon as she calls her dog to cross the river the dog does it without getting wet. How is this possible?

32. What day of the week do chickens fear the most?

33. What did the poor horse say when he fell over?

34. What do you call a pig with no legs?

_____

35. What did the chicken say when she bought her new lipstick?

_____

36. Why does a milk stall used to milk cows only have 3 legs?

_____

37. Where's a sheeps' favorite holiday destination?

_____

38. What time does the duck wake up?

_____

39. Name an animal that can honk without a horn?

_____

40. What do you call when you shave a crazy sheep

_____

41. What do you call a cross between a chicken and a cow?

_____

42. If a human was to carry the burden I have to carry they would surely break their back. I'm not rich but I do leave silver in my track. What animal am I?

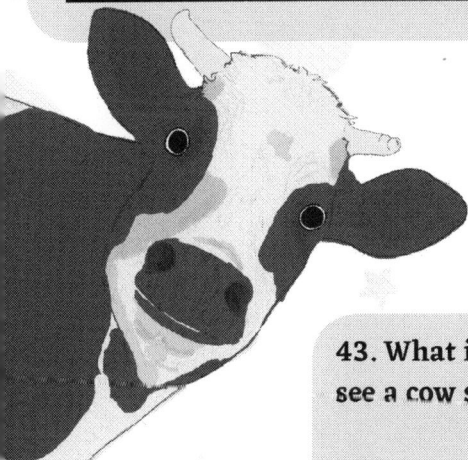

_____

43. What is it known as when you see a cow spying on another cow?

_____

44. What do you call a horse that lives next door to you?

_____

45. You might be called this animal if you're afraid. Which animal is this?

_____

46. The start of me goes on toast and the end of me is usually how birds move. Which animal am I?

_____

47. What animal goes into the water black but comes out red?

_____

48. What peels like an onion but still remains whole?

_____

49. What did the turkey say to the rooster when he challenged him to a fight?

_____

50. What animal has a mane that can give you a nasty bite but is certainly not related to cats?

_____

51. I am a busy sort of creature. I very much like burying my treasure in the ground so I can come and collect it once winter approaches. My tail is big a fluffy and you will probably spot me running away from you up a tree. What am I?

_____

52. I'm a royal sort of cat and I take pride in my appearance. What animal am I?

_____

CHAPTER 6: ANAGRAMS

An anagram is where a word, words or phrases letters can be rearranged to give a brand new word. Next up we have a collection of easy, moderate and hard anagrams that will be sure to give your brain a good testing. As always with riddles, before you write your answer down have a good think about the clues you've been given in the question and make sure you rearranged word fits what the question is asking.

Right, are you ready!? Let's get into some fun anagrams!

EASY LEVEL ANAGRAMS

1. SLIP into 1 word describing a feature of the human body.

   _____

2. USE into 1 word that is someone's name

   _____

3. WOLF into in 1 word that describes something a river does

   _____

4. PEA into 1 word which describes a close human relative.

   _____

5. TONE into 1 word that describes something that you would use a pen to do.

_____

6. SKIN into 1 word that would describe what would happen to a ship with a large hole in it.

_____

7. CAFE into 1 word that you always have on you but are never able to see without a reflection.

_____

8. ACRE into 1 word which is used to describe when people run as fast they can against each other

_____

9. RAW into 1 word which describes when large groups of people fight each other.

_____

10. MEATS into 1 word is created when you heat water to high temperatures.

_____

11. TAB into 1 word which baseball players couldn't live without.

_____

12. ACT into 1 word which links together lions, tigers and cheetahs.

_____

13. RING into 1 word which describes which describes a kind of smile.

_____

14. TAR into an animal which you wouldn't want in your house.

_____

15. RACE into 1 word which describes the act of looking after someone.

_____

16. BINARY into 1 word which describes someone who is rather clever.

_____

17. INCH into 1 word which describes a human feature.

---

18. GLEAN into 1 word which describes a non-human creature that brings peace and harmony.

---

19. RAMS into 1 word which doesn't describe earth but something similar.

---

20. SILENT into 1 word which describes what the things on the side of your head are for.

---

21. REMOTE into something which is in outer space and we really don't want to come to earth.

---

22. REAP into a fruit.

---

23. ROBED into 1 word which you probably get when you're doing homework!

_____

24. VOTES into 1 word which describes something in the kitchen which gets hot.

_____

25. CIDER into 1 word that describes a sad emotion.

_____

26. BELOW into 1 word that is one of the parts of your own body that you can't touch with your tongue.

_____

27. LAMP into 1 word which describes another part of your body but this time thinks hands.

_____

28. DESSERTS into 1 word which would potentially describe how you feel when you're studying for an important test.

_____

29. OURS into 1 word which describes a type of delicious candy.

_____

30. BEAK into 1 word describing what you need to do to cake mixture in order to eat it

_____

MEDIUM LEVEL ANAGRAMS

Time to increase the difficult now. The next 10 riddles are story based riddles and will require a bit more thinking to solve them.

Good luck!

1. Mia loved to bake cakes with her mom every Wednesday afternoon after school had finished. Baking cakes was fun but she always had to make sure the mixture was the right consistency, otherwise it wouldn't work. Mia would always bake the cakes in the kitchen. Rearrange the letters in KITCHEN to spell the word which describes what consistency Mia was looking for that isn't too runny.

_____

2. Tom's favorite fruit is a MELON. Chris's is a strawberry and Gina's is a banana. Tom, Chris and Gina are all very surprised by Richard's favorite food as it's not very sweet. Gina is a bright spark and spots that if you rearrange the letters of Tom's favorite fruit you get Richard's favorite fruit. What is Richard's favorite fruit?

_____

3. A school class was going on a school trip abroad to the wonderful country of France. They were going to be staying in the capital city of France which is Paris. There were 30 of them in the class which means they all had a partner each. Rearrange the letters in the word PARIS to make a word describing how the children partnered up with each other.

_____

4. Devon lives in California and loves activities on the water. He lives 30 minutes from the coast which is where he always does water-based activities. His favorite activity of them all is canoeing. Rearrange the word CANOE to spell what Devon is canoeing on.

_____

5. Leo the Lion was the most scary lion in all of Africa and he had quite the temper. All the other animals thought he was really mean to them. Rearrange the word MEAN to spell out one of Leo's obvious physical features?

_____

6. "WHAT the heck" screamed Tracey, who just saw a frozen pig eat a dragon covered in ketchup and couldn't believe her eyes. Tracey quickly opened her eyes and was thankful it was just a rather strange dream. Rearrange the word WHAT to spell the word which describes what would happen to the frozen pig if it stayed on in the sun too long?

_____

7. You have 5 senses: touch, hearing, sight, smell and taste. Rearrange the word TASTE to spell a word which would accurately describe Ohio.

_____

8. This is a made up fact, are you ready? The more cows there are on this specific side of the country, the more beef stew people tend to make. Rearrange the word STEW to figure out the side of the country.

_____

9. Harry Potter is known for being a wizard at Hogwarts. At the crack of dawn every morning, he would have to get up and make sure he packed his bag for school. Rearrange the word DAWN to spell a very important item that all wizards should have if they want to be successful.

_____

10. Lucinda has until recently been having some trouble getting to sleep. Luckily for her in just the last two weeks she has been doing this one special "thing" before going to bed to allow her to get to sleep. Rearrange the word THING to spell the word which describes something to do with sleep.

_____

HARD LEVEL ANAGRAMS

Now, let's really test your brain skills here with the hard level anagrams. All of these anagrams are phrases which need to be rearranged.

Good luck!

1. Rearrange AMEN STORIES to spell 1 word which describes a place where a religious person may pray.

_____

2. Rearrange RUNS A TREAT to spell 1 word that describes a place that might be good to eat at.

_____

3. Rearrange I'M A DOT IN PLACE to spell 3 words that describe something that you can put between two numbers.

_____

4. Rearrange GOLDEN LAND to spell 2 words, which if you take the opposite of the first word, would describe a few states in the north east of the US.

_____

5. Rearrange BUILT TO STAY FREE to spell 3 words which describe a famous monument in America.

_____

6. Rearrange A TRUE SIGN into 1 word which describes something people add at the end of written letters.

_____

7. Rearrange MAY IT END into 1 word that describes a very explosive material used in years gone by.

_____

8. Rearrange TWELVE PLUS ONE into 3 words which equal exactly the same value.

_____

9. Rearrange HERE COME DOTS into 2 words which spell out a very important World War 2 invention.

_____

10. Rearrange GRAND OLD EVILS into 3 words which spell two very precious materials we all would want more of.

_____

11. Rearrange HE IN NET SPORT into 3 words which describe someone who is very good at a racket sport.

_____

12. Rearrange THAT QUEER SHAKE into 2 words which describe and natural occurrence that would leaving you shaking.

_____

13. Rearrange VOICES RANT ON into 1 word which describes when two people are speaking with each other.

_____

14. Rearrange A YEAR TO SHUT DOWN into 3 words which describe an event that people thought was going to happen in 2000.

_____

15. Rearrange I AM NOT ACTIVE to spell 2 words which describe when you are not at school.

_____

16. Rearrange AN OLD GUY to spell 2 words which are the opposite to this.

_____

17. Rearrange NO CITY DUST HERE to spell 2 two words that describe a place that certainly wouldn't have any city dust and is far away from a city.

_____

18. Rearrange MOON STARER to spell 2 words that describe someone who enjoys staring into the night sky.

_____

19. Rearrange WORTH TEA into 2 words that spell something very important to make a good cup of tea.

_____

20. Rearrange THE CLASSROOM to spell 2 words which would describe someone who is very much in charge of the classroom.

_____

WELL DONE! You've just finished your 333rd question in this ultimate book of riddles, brain-teasers and anagrams!

I hope you have enjoyed working through them and they have been a good test of your "riddling" abilities.

If you've enjoyed this book I would love to know!

ASK YOUR PARENTS, if you could be so kind to head over to Amazon and leave either a star rating or a short written review for it. It helps me to compete with the big publishers and let me know how to improve future books!

Simply scan the QR code below, and it will take you the review page. Your support is so appreciated!

★★★★★

1. An egg
2. Finlay
3. Envelope
4. Every month except February
5. A cold
6. A towel
7. A refrigerator
8. Eyes
9. Black Bear
10. Trick question – it depends on the year they were born!
11. A clock
12. 'S' is the only capital letter in Spain
13. Short
14. Incorrectly
15. Wet
16. The letter 'G'
17. A carrot
18. Libraries
19. An echo
20. Rain
21. Silence
22. A book
23. Alphabet
24. Race car
25. Fire
26. Ice cube
27. He fell off the bottom step
28. Postbox office
29. The letter 'N'
30. None. Noah rescued the animals on the ark – not Moses!
31. A hole
32. A deck of cards
33. The future
34. Corn
35. NOON
36. Queue
37. A rubber band

38. A map
39. A trash can
40. Your right elbow
41. Grandpa was bald
42. The moon
43. It's lid
44. The corner
45. Popcorn
46. Teapot
47. A refrigerator
48. GONE - Add the letter 'G' to the start of the word
49. A stamp
50. A keyboard
51. He has a $10 bill
52. Leapfrog
53. Ad-dress
54. The world wide web
55. A spelling bee
56. A cereal killer
57. Running out of gas
58. Because a B (bee) always comes after them
59. A snailor
60. He had no-"body" to go with

1. Noise
2. A coin
3. Christopher Colombus
4. Your name
5. Lifeguard
6. Stars
7. A sponge
8. A snowman
9. Piano
10. Watermelon
11. Beehive
12. A wheel
13. Woman - (man and Oman)
14. Parrot
15. Gloves
16. The letter 'R'
17. A tooth
18. Clouds
19. A compass
20. A bed
21. A promise
22. A candle
23. Money
24. Dentist
25. I'm a barber
26. Cutlery
27. Telephone
28. Mercury
29. A hole
30. A chair
31. A battery
32. An airplane
33. A river
34. The letter 'E'
35. Pea
36. Electric fan
37. Water
38. Mirror

39. Age
40. I'm a candle
41. A breath
42. A joke
43. Hot air balloon
44. A chicken in an egg
45. Carpet
46. A heart
47. A tree
48. A fence
49. Calendar
50. Ice
51. Dozens - 1 dozen is 12!
52. A needle
53. Christmas tree
54. A chair
55. A ruler
56. Grapes
57. A milk truck
58. Parking lot
59. A bar of soap
60. Sticky tape

1. 11 years old. When Lucy was 10 her brother was half her age which would have made him 5 at the time, so there is a 5 year difference between them. She is now 16, so 16 - 5 = 11, which is how old her brother is.

2. There were actually only 3 people fishing so each of them got 2 fish. There was one father and his son, and finally the grandson, which makes 2 fathers and 2 sons!

3. None of them - they all weigh a ton!

4. Their aunt is Liam's mom!

5. Seven

6. Today is January 1st and Charlotte's birthday is the 31st of December. Charlotte was 9 the day before yesterday (December 30th), then turned 10 the next day. This year on December 31st she'll turn 11, so next year she'll turn 12.

7. She has 8 kids. She has 6 sons and 2 daughters.

8. It's midnight – of course there will be no sun in the sky!

9. 5! You have taken 5 out of the bowl. The question was "how many potato chunks do YOU have?" Not how many does the bowl have!

10. A decimal point. 5.8 is both greater than 5 and less than 7.

11. $25 - Their pricing method is $5 for every letter an item has. We told you it was strange.

12. $26. $10 for every vowel an item contains it and $2 for every consonant an item contains.

13. Turn it upside down. 108 = 6 X 18

14. 1, 2 and 3. 1 + 2 + 3 = 6 AND 1 X 2 X 3 = 6.

15. Any number. If a number is doubled and then multiplied by 4, its actually been multiplied by 8 so dividing it by 8 will actually just give you the original number again, it doesn't matter which one.

16. Just the same 3 chickens. They produce eggs at a constant rate so you only need your 3 trusty chickens!

17. 44 + 4 4 = 45. 4 4 =1 and therefore 44 + 1 = 45

18. I am talking about time. 6am + 7 = 1pm.

19. 0. If you multiply any number by 0 you will always get 0.

20. Two minutes. It will take 1 minute for the nose to pass through the tunnel and then another minute for the last carriage to travel through the tunnel.

21. $30 each. An Ostrich has 2 legs which means each leg is worth $7.5 ($15 total). So 7.5 X 4 = 30.

22. He took away the 'F' and 'E' from five to be left with IV - roman numeral four.

23. 18 apples, 6 pears, 12 melons. Start with melons first of all as we know he has as many melons as there are months in the year which is 12. You can then work out the pears by doing 12 divided by 2 which gives you 6 pears, as we know he has half as many pears as melons. Finally you can work out the apples by multiplying 6 X 3 as we know he has three times as many apples as pears, so 6 X 3.

24. Dimensions. A cube has 3 dimensions, a circle has 2 dimensions and a point has 0 dimensions.

25. 50%. It's a coin which means there is a 50% probability every time you flip, and it doesn't matter what the previous results were.

26. An oval.

27. A minus (-) sign. 666 - 66 = 600

28. None of these statements are correct. 13 plus 19 and 19 plus 13 both equal 32, AND 19 minus 13 = 6.

29. $0 - roosters are a male chickens and therefore don't lay eggs.

30. 0. The keypad has a 0 in it which means the number will always be 0.

31. You need to cut the pizza 4 times. When you cut the pizza in half once, you divide it in two. When you slice it two times you get 4 slices, when you slice it 3 times you get 6 slices and you guessed it...... slicing it 4 times will give you 8 pizza slices!

32. 100 loaves of bread. A dozen is 12 and for $1.20 you can get 12 loaves of bread which makes each individual loaf of bread $0.10. You now need to divide $10 by $0.10, the easiest way to do this if you convert them both to cents. There are 100 cents in 1 dollar, so 10 dollars equals 1000 cents (10 x 100). You then need to divide 1000 by 10 cents, to get 100 loaves.

33. $27. The old chicken will lay 3 eggs in 9 days (1 egg every 3 days). Young chickens will lay 36 eggs in 9 days (2 X 9 = 18 eggs for 1 chicken. 18 X 2 = 36 eggs for two chickens). Ducks will lay 18 eggs in 9 days (9 X 2 = 18).
   3 + 36 + 18 = 57 eggs total.
   57 - 3 = 54 eggs (3 eggs were broken)
   54 X $0.50 = $27

34. He was born in 1998 B.C. You count time backwards - 1980 B.C. is 18 years after 1998 B.C.

35. 16 days. You would think it would be 20 days as he is able to slowly climb 2 meters every day. On the first day the slug reaches 2 meters, the second day 4 meters etc. On day 15 the slug reaches 30 meters. On day 16 the slug climbs 10 meters and reaches 40 meters, doesn't fall back down and escapes the pit.

36. 8

37. 7. Half of 2 is 1, 1 + 2 + 2 + 2 = 7

38. $105. It's not $110 as you may have been thinking. $105 + $5 = $110 whereas $110 + $10 = $120.

39. 161

40. 14 matches of tennis. William won 9 matches. 5 wins cancel out George's 5 wins, and then William won 4 more to win the 4 burgers. 9 + 5 = 14 matches total.

41. 19 times - (8, 18, 28, 38, 48, 58, 68, 78, 80, 81, 82, 83, 84, 85, 86, 87, 88, 89, 98)

42. 6 pounds (3 x 12 / 6 = 6)

43. They both weigh the same. There are 16 ounces in 1 pound.

44. Sid is awake and crawling for 9 hours of the day, the rest of the time he is sleeping. If he crawls at 50 cm per hour, he will crawl a total of 450 cm in 9 hours (50 X 9). 450 cm converted into meters is 4.5 meters, as there are 100 cm in 1 meter.

45. 1489. Second digit could either be 4, 3 or 2, as these are the only numbers that can be multiplied by 2 without exceeding single digits. 4-3=1, 3-3=0, and 2-3=-1. We can rule out -1, and 0, so we know the first digit is 1 and the second digit is 4. Now let's add 7 to the first digit. This gives us 8 as the 3rd digit. Thus, the number is 1489!

46. 16 chairs. The same four men could build 8 chairs in 8 hours (4 X 2). If you double the amount of men, you can simply double the amount of chairs, so you will get 16 chairs.

47. It will be cheaper to take two friends just once as he will only have to buy 3 tickets. If he goes with just one friend once he will have to buy 4 tickets - 2 for 2 friends, and 2 himself.

48. Fruits = 198 and Vegetables = 24

First of all you need to know your fruits and vegetables.

Total fruit Isabella bought - 20 + 120 + 80 = 220 fruits

Total vegetable Isabella bought - 24 + 6 = 30

10% of 220 is 22. Then subtract 22 from 220, which equals 198. She has 198 fruits left.

Then for the vegetables: 20% of 30 = 6, and 30 - 6 = 24!

49. 2 pounds. You might have thought 1.5 pounds but that is wrong. The bag of candy weighs one pound, plus half of a bag, the one pound gives you the weight of the other half of the bag. As half a bag weighs one pound, the entire bag weighs two pounds. Yes, that was a tricky one!

50. 500 legs in total!

Lion legs = 12 X 4 = 48

Wild dog legs = 14 X 4 = 56

Ostrich legs = 2 X 2 = 4

Wildebeest legs = 98 X 4 = 392

51. 1/4

52. 11. 8 has 2 circles within the numbers it which means 88 = 4. 9 has 1 circle in it which means 99 only equals 2. There are 11 circles in 809689609!

53. Add the number 1 at the end of 100 and you get 1001.

54. $61.50

First we need to work out how much Mom is paying. So we need to add the cost of the shoes and sweater together; $20 + $40.50 = $60.50. Mom is paying half of this, so we need to divide 60.50 by 2 = $30.25. You are paying the other half of these two items which means you'll be paying $30.25. The final thing to do is to add $30.25 to $31.25 (cost of the top) to see how much you will be paying overall. $31.25 + $30.25 = $61.50

55. 1,500 ft. First of all, you need to convert 10 hours into minutes - 10 hours = 600 minutes. Then do 600 divided by 40 to get 15 (this tells you he can walk 100 feet, 15 times, if it takes him 40 minutes each 100 feet. Then simply multiply 100 ft X 15 to get 1500ft in 10 hours!

56. 124 chocolate bars in total. 14 X 9 = 126. Then you have to simply subtract 2 from 126 as there were two missing from one of the boxes. So the total is 124.

57. 5 hours and 30 minutes

58. 6:28am. Add all the numbers in the question together as they all involve time which it will take him to get up, ready and to work on this day. 10 + 3 + 50 + 19 + 10 = 92 minutes. Subtract 92 minutes from 8am and you get 6:28am.

59. 11850. 2300 + 4500 = 6800. The third year produced 550 more than the second year. This would mean that 5050 were produced in the third year. 5050 + 6800 = 11850 total.

60. $24

First of all we need to add together the total sum of everything he bought. Chips = $9, chicken = $12, candy = $2.50, and yogurt = $5. 9 + 12 + 2.5 + 5 = 28.50.
You then need to add this to what change he had left - 28.50 plus 15.50 = 44.
Finally, subtract the original amount from this amount - 44 - 20 = 24 He withdrew $24 from his bank.

ANSWERS: CHAPTER 4, FUNNY RIDDLES

1. Anything can jump higher than a building duh! Buildings can't jump, their buildings!
2. A pumpkin patch of course!
3. Poop
4. Your fingers
5. Hot dog
6. Frostbite
7. They're always stuffed
8. Lost!
9. Dasher
10. Stop imagining
11. Because they put out the salsa
12. A goldfish
13. Hip Hop
14. "Ketchup!"
15. To the dock
16. You're pointless
17. A mushroom
18. It was full of problems
19. Nice belt you got there
20. Jelly beans
21. The elf-abet
22. Sham-boo!
23. It's full of Cheetahs!
24. Twister
25. With experi - mints
26. Stop picking on me
27. She was a little 'hoarse' today
28. They always 'quack' the case!
29. It ran out of juice
30. A garbage truck
31. She wanted to see time fly
32. A dino-snore
33. The teacher told him it was a piece of cake
34. "C" AND "Y"
35. It wasn't raining today
36. PI
37. Fungi - Fun-Guys!
38. Your tongue
39. Your legs
40. He wanted to find Pooh!

1. A bookworm
2. Kangaroo
3. Porcupine
4. It saw the oceans bottom
5. They prefer to hunt knights
6. The window is closed
7. A computer mouse
8. Because pepper makes them sneeze
9. Because they have 9 lives
10. A sad zebra
11. "That hit the spot!"
12. They both have scales
13. A bat
14. A water bed
15. The horse works on a mill and walks in a circular pattern
16. Donkey and monkey
17. A whale
18. A rhino
19. A giraffes shadow
20. None of them as you can't get an apple from a pineapple tree
21. 'You've read my mind!'
22. A bear
23. In a tie
24. A deer
25. I already have a bill
26. The Elephant
27. An Owl
28. Peregrine Falcon
29. A Gorilla
30. To the retail store
31. The river was frozen
32. Fry-days
33. Help! I've fallen and can't giddyup!
34. A groundhog
35. Put it on my bill
36. Because the cow has the 'udder' - other!
37. The Baaaahamas
38. The quack of dawn
39. A goose
40. Sheer madness
41. Roost beef

ANSWERS: CHAPTER 5, ANIMAL RIDDLES CONT...

42. A snail
43. A steak out
44. A Neigh-bor
45. A chicken
46. Butterfly
47. Lobster
48. Lizard
49. "Are you a chicken?"
50. A horse
51. A squirrel
52. Lion

ANSWERS: CHAPTER 6, ANAGRAMS (EASY)

1. Lips
2. Sue
3. Flow
4. Ape
5. Note
6. Sink
7. Face
8. Race
9. War
10. Steam
11. Bat
12. Cat
13. Grin
14. Rat
15. Care
16. Brainy
17. Chin
18. Angel
19. Mars
20. Listen
21. Meteor
22. Pear
23. Bored

ANSWERS: CHAPTER 6, ANAGRAMS (EASY) CONT...

24. Stove
25. Cried
26. Elbow
27. Palm
28. Stressed
29. Sour
30. Bake

ANSWERS: CHAPTER 6, ANAGRAMS (MEDIUM)

1. Thicken
2. Lemon
3. Pairs
4. Ocean
5. Mane
6. Thaw
7. State
8. West
9. Wand
10. Night

ANSWERS: CHAPTER 6, ANAGRAMS (HARD)

1. Monasteries
2. Restaurant
3. A Decimal Point
4. Old England
5. Statue of Liberty
6. Signature
7. Dynamite
8. Eleven plus two
9. The Morse Code
10. Gold and Silver

ANSWERS: CHAPTER 6, ANAGRAMS (HARD)

11. The Tennis Pro
12. The earthquakes
13. Conversation
14. Year Two Thousand
15. Vacation Time
16. Young Lady
17. The Countryside
18. Astronomer
19. Hot water
20. Schoolmaster

WHAT DID YOU THINK OF THE BOOK?

As with every book I release I genuinely have so much fun putting all the questions together. I very much hope you enjoyed it.

If you found the book enjoyable it would be very much appreciated if you either left a star rating or a short and sweet written review on Amazon. (This helps me to compete against the big publishers out there).

How To Leave a review on Amazon:
- Go to this books page on Amazon - you can find it by typing in the title to Amazon
- Scroll halfway down the page until you see 'Write a Customer Review'
- Click on that button and it will let you either leave a star rating or you can choose to leave a written review

OTHER BOOKS BY AC BROOKER

If you've enjoyed this book I've got a ton of other books on Amazon if you want to check them out. Here's a full list:

- The Ultimate Book of Riddles and Brain Teasers for Adults and Kids
- The Ultimate Large Print Word Search for Adults and Seniors
- Christmas Songs Word Search
- The Ultimate Book of Sudoku (3 in 1 collection)

I also have a selection of interesting facts book on Audible. If you type in my name to audible you will be able to find them there.

FREE BOOK GROUP!

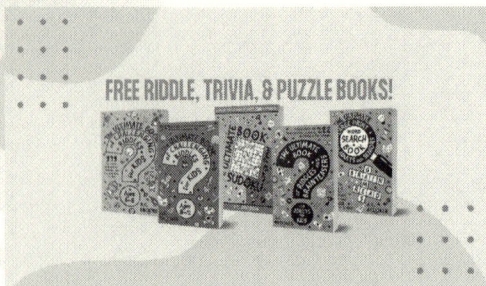

FREE RIDDLE, TRIVIA, & PUZZLE BOOKS!

Scan the QR code below to get added to our next book mailed to you for FREE!

Made in United States
Troutdale, OR
06/07/2023